# FEBRUARY PETALS

ANKITA SINGH

Copyright © Ankita Singh
All Rights Reserved.

This book has been self-published with all reasonable efforts taken to make the material error-free by the author. No part of this book shall be used, reproduced in any manner whatsoever without written permission from the author, except in the case of brief quotations embodied in critical articles and reviews.

The Author of this book is solely responsible and liable for its content including but not limited to the views, representations, descriptions, statements, information, opinions and references ["Content"]. The Content of this book shall not constitute or be construed or deemed to reflect the opinion or expression of the Publisher or Editor. Neither the Publisher nor Editor endorse or approve the Content of this book or guarantee the reliability, accuracy or completeness of the Content published herein and do not make any representations or warranties of any kind, express or implied, including but not limited to the implied warranties of merchantability, fitness for a particular purpose. The Publisher and Editor shall not be liable whatsoever for any errors, omissions, whether such errors or omissions result from negligence, accident, or any other cause or claims for loss or damages of any kind, including without limitation, indirect or consequential loss or damage arising out of use, inability to use, or about the reliability, accuracy or sufficiency of the information contained in this book.

Made with ♥ on the Notion Press Platform
www.notionpress.com

*The book entitled February petals is dedicated to divine Goddess Saraswati , her blessings on my writing skills inspired me to write this book.*

*The book is dedicated to my Parents Mrs. Madhu Yadav and Mr. Hemant Kumar their blessings inspired me to write this book.*

# Contents

# Preface

*The month of February ,*

*Holds the dignity.*

*dignity of love ,*

*As a pure dove......*

*Hence this book entitled " February Petals " is bunch of poetry blossoms , to define dignity of self love and respect....*

*Happy February to all readers of this book.*

*- Ankita Singh*

# Acknowledgements

*My heartiest thanks to my Mother Mrs. Madhu Yadav , her adorable teachings of humanity in life inspired me to write poems on love for nature. My heartiest thanks to my father Mr. Hemant Kumar his guidance in every step of life made me to think, reflect and understand each tiny phenomena, ups and downs , lesson to admire my dignity and self respect and use them as a topics of poetry in arena of my writings.*

*My heartiest thanks to publishers to publish my manuscript in book format.*

# Author Introduction

Ankita Singh

*Ankita Singh is indie author and freelance writer native to Lucknow , Uttar Pradesh, India. She was born on 10 February , so she has special attachment with this particular month. Her 170 poems has been published in reputed books and magazines.*

*After completing her graduation in Mass communication and video production she has earned degrees in Masters in journalism and Mass communication, B. Ed, M. Ed from university of Lucknow. Her thrist for education further encouraged her to pursue M. A. English and M. A. Education from Dr. Ram Manohar Lohia Avadh University, Ayodhya, Uttar Pradesh .She has qualified UGC NET in subject education 6 times.*

*Till now her 18 books entitled " Kalam ke palash, chahakte panne, savan ke Hastakshar " Rangeen khidkiyan , Kavya ke Basant as a collection of her poems in hindi , Poetic Feathers and Musings of perfect Moonlight as poetry collection in English.*

*"shunya sarovar , sneh Taru " books on short stories hindi edition, "Ability daffodils : Inclusive education strategies to teach children with Disabilities , Tenses : The blossoms of English grammar " based on english curriculum, further sparrows Fiesta as a reference book English edition, and four other books related to related to curriculum ,"festive candles based on art and photography has been published. Her area of interest includes educational psychology and research in education. A delight towards glittering lights makes her to play with wax and make decorative candles. To touch the humanistic approach of her life, main aim of Author is to provide love, care and healthy environment to stray animals to survive with dignity on earth.*

# 1. My soul will shine.....

*My valentine is mother earth,*

*I know it's worth ...*

*It's greenery gratitude my hearts ..*

*mother earth*

*Just like happiness , full of joy kart.*

*Thus , to celebrate this valentine*

*My soul will shine ,*

*My soul will shine,*

*To plant a banyan tree.*

*Which Provides oxygen for free.*

*My valentine is Little dog ,*

*He is snowy fog ,*

*In hotty summer noon .*

*To cherish me like a boon.*

*Hence , this valentine*

*My soul will shine,*

*My soul will shine,*

*To feed stray canine .*

*And say dear you are my Valentine...*

*- Ankita Singh*

# 2. Shrinking Humanity

*Love is to praise earth ,*

*A Real vision*

*To understand it's worth .*

*Love is to plant trees,*

*A booster Dose ,*

*To provide oxygen for free.*

*Love is to care stray canine.*

*To hold its paw and say-*

*Oh ! My charm You are my valentine.*

*Love is to praise rain .*

*To cherish it's presence ,*

*And forget pain .*

*Love is to adore nature .*

*To thank mother earth,*

*And love every creature.*

*Love is to feed birds of surroundings.*

*Birds of surroundings*

*Spread greenery ....*

*As token of Happy boundings.*

*Love is to preserve environment.*

*As a task of real worth.*

*Which is most significant.*

*It's all about love,*

*To shine as moon .*

*To admire earth resources ,*

*As a boon....*

*In midnight as stars.*

*For removing all scars ,*

*From soul of shrinking humanity.*

*Ankita Singh*

# 3. Platonic love.....

*Platonic love is ,*

*Sign to love inner heart and soul.*

*Just to sow a seed of responsible role .*

*To cherish each other's presence ,*

*As a soulmate ,*

*To love each other in every pleasure .*

*A pleasure of youth .*

*A pleasure of old age .*

*A pleasure to fly .*

*A pleasure to cage .*

*A pleasure to joy .*

*A pleasure to cry.*

*A pleasure to explore .*

*A pleasure to shy.*

*A pleasure to forget.*

*A pleasure to regret.*

*A pleasure to enjoy pure love .*

*Is a platonic love.*

*To cherish purity of life .*

*purity of life*

*And propose my soul to enjoy my presence .*

*In light of self love*

*In light of self love..*

*- Ankita Singh*

# 4. In light of my choice...

*Love is light*

*It shines all bright ...*

*If enlightened with self love*

*Just to cherish as dove ...*

*To respect self goals.*

*As a dignified role ....*

*To appreciate my gains.*

*To appreciate my pains.*

*To hold my boat ,*

*In flood of rains.*

*To regain lost me...*

*Just to see*

*Just to see*

*My self in shadow of love*

*Love for my inner voice.*

Inner voice

*To choose independent me ,*

*In light of my choice.*

*In light of my choice...*

*Ankita Singh*

# 5. Love as I experienced .....

*Love as I experienced*

*Is love for nature .*

*To respect every creature.*

*A love document signed to plant tree,*

Tree

*That provide oxygen for free.*

*A love document signed to enjoy rain drops.*

*Appreciate farmers ,to sow kindness crops.*

*A love document signed to feed stray canine,*

*And say dear you are my valentine.*

*A love document signed to praise Greenery ...*

*Just to enjoy earth's natural sceneray .*

*A love document signed to enjoy love flame .*

*In fire of heart's game .*

*Just to write love song .*

*For environment and earth.*

*And celebrate its million dollar worth .*

*- Ankita Singh*

# 6. To simple me ...

*Love is token of self respect*

*To relinquish term we*

*Just to shine shine shine,*

*In shadow of mine .*

*A token of self realization.*

*A token of self determination.*

*A token of self power .*

*A charm to shower.*

*Best wishes of independent me .*

*To simple me .*

*- Ankita Singh*

# 7. Listen girls

*Love is to sing*

*Lyrics of your wings*

*From Which you can fly ,*

*So high in sky.*

*In galaxy of self respect.*

*Just to reject ....*

*Unwanted choice ,*

*Enforced upon you .*

*Embedded with hidden clue.*

*That -*

*Oh dear ! She is just girl*

*Not a pearl ...*

*To preserve her in garland*

*Give her a fairy land .*

*Where she can stand ,*

*Is still weird .*

*Oh girl , go can destroy such rules.*

Listen Girls

*You are not a materialistic tools.*

*You have your own choice ,*

*You have your own voice.*

*You can sing love song.*

*For your dignity too stand strong.....*

*You can sing love song.*

*For your decision to stand strong...*

*Dear girls , you are gold.*

*Choose your choice as you are bold .*

*Ankita Singh*

# 8. Self fame

*Love is choice*

*Of choosing self.*

*Self love.*

*Self respect.*

*Self determination*

*Self realization.*

*Self dependency.*

***Self reliability.***

***Self values.***

***Self roles.***

***Self goals.***

Self goals

*Just to achieve a fame.*

*A token of love to ,*

*Admire your name.*

*Love is game ,*

*Of self fame .....*

*Of self fame.....*

*Ankita Singh*

# 9. In beauty of our own fragrance.

*Love is a dove*

*Of pure feather.*

*A symbol to just gather ,*

*Feelings of our emotion ...*

*As signature of heart' s promotion,*

*A token to feel for someone .*

*A token to feel for something.*

*And to get nothing ,*

*In return...*

*It's just to earn ....*

*Emptiness of life...*

*Love is art,*

*To draw a emotion,*

*On empty canvas of life...*

*To revive self realisation*

*As booster of soul' s manifestation .*

*A token to remember nothing,*

*A token to forget everything...*

*And admire self presence,*

*In beauty of our own fragrance.*

*In beauty of our own fragrance.*

*Ankita Singh*

# 10. In charm of fame...

*Love is a rhyme ,*

*A good wish of moon's Hyme.*

Moon

*Enchanted to shine ..*

*The thorns of my pine.*

*And say yes I'm fine ,*

*Alone .*

*Ready to live lone.*

*Just like moon.*

*In clusters of stars .*

*I my self will remove my scars .*

*Scars of defects .*

*Just to reflect ,*

*My loneliness is my sword ,*

*Ready to cut cord,*

*Of fake people .*

*Of fake hopes.*

*And enjoy the slopes ,*

*The Slopes of my life,*

*As up and down .*

*Just a pledge to regain my crown .*

*Reflecting my name ,*

*In charm of self love ,*

*In charm of fame...*

*Ankita Singh*

# 11. Message from an Independent girl .....

*Love is name plate ,*

*On hearts gate.*

*Reflecting my name .*

*In ocean of fame.*

*Is Hyme of self care .*

*Ready to dare ,*

*Harsh waves of social sea .....*

*Who cannot see.....*

*My Independence.*

*I'm ready to defense ,*

*For my "I" ,*

*To say good bye we .*

*Now I will care only for me.*

*- Ankita Singh*

# 12. Better alone !

*Hats off to every Strom*

*Oh dear !*

*You made me strong .*

*Strong enough to stand alone .*

*At life's road that is too lone.*

Lone Road

*Keen to mend torn pieces of me.*

*Trying to hold I & let go social we.*

*Forever , forever , forever.*

*To wipe my eyes & cry never.*

*For anything.*

*Wishing to spread my tiny wings .*

*Just to fly high*

*To say big good bye.*

*For who ever I was life's darkest zone.*

*You may leave ! i'am better alone.*

*Ankita Singh*

# 13. Definition of self love

*self love is a sign,*

*Which you can define..*

*A mark embraked on -*

*Sailing soul ....*

*In ocean of intimacy.*

*A note of Conspiracy.*

*To steal one's own heart.*

*Which no one can depart .*

*Just from departure of physical world.*

*Love is platonic ....it can be felt.*

*Ankita Singh*

# 14. Can't be tamed

*Her wings are strong enough to fly .*

*Dedicated to achieve a goal too high.*

*She can touch the success sky.*

*Oh ! World you don't tell lie i.e*

*She is women she can't try.*

*She is bold,*

*Her tears are dry.*

*Her wings are meant only to fly .*

*So high , so high .*

*In galaxy of fame.*

*Cherished to earn her name.*

*So dear don't play game.*

*She is tigress can't be tamed.*

*Ankita Singh*

# 15. Ready to earn fame....

*Oh! What I did ?*

*Oh ! What I did ?*

*Just wasted time .*

*In name of false aspirations.*

*In name of depression.*

*Now it's time for celebration .*

*To enjoy " I" insted of social " we"*

*So I can see*

*My fluttering wings,*

*Flying too high .*

*To achieve sky.*

*A sky of my name.*

*Ready to earn fame.*

*Ready to earn fame.*

*Ankita Singh*

# Contact Details

Email id - anks26.as@gmail.com

Instagram id - @anki.ta7662

# Thank You

*My humble thanks to Goddess Saraswati , who in entire preperation of manuscript has inspired me and kept me motivated to timely finish the project.*

9 798889 519713

Printed by Libri Plureos GmbH in Hamburg, Germany